PEARL HARBOR

Written by

DAVID BOYD

Illustrated by

DREW NG

ALISON QUIGLEY

MITSUO FUCHIDA

JASMINE OBASAN

BUDDY STOCKTON

DR. FUJIRO OBASAN

REAL PEOPLE IN HISTORY

MITSUO FUCHIDA (1902-1976): A Japanese military commander who led the attack on Pearl Harbor.

FICTIONAL CHARACTERS

ALISON QUIGLEY: A 12-year-old girl whose father is a U.S. fleet navy captain at Pearl Harbor.

JASMINE OBASAN: A 12-year-old Japanese girl who becomes a good friend of Alison.

BUDDY STOCKTON: Alison's friend and classmate, and son of a U.S. fleet navy captain at Pearl Harbor.

DR. FUJIRO OBASAN: A famous Japanese poet, and Jasmine's father.

Contents

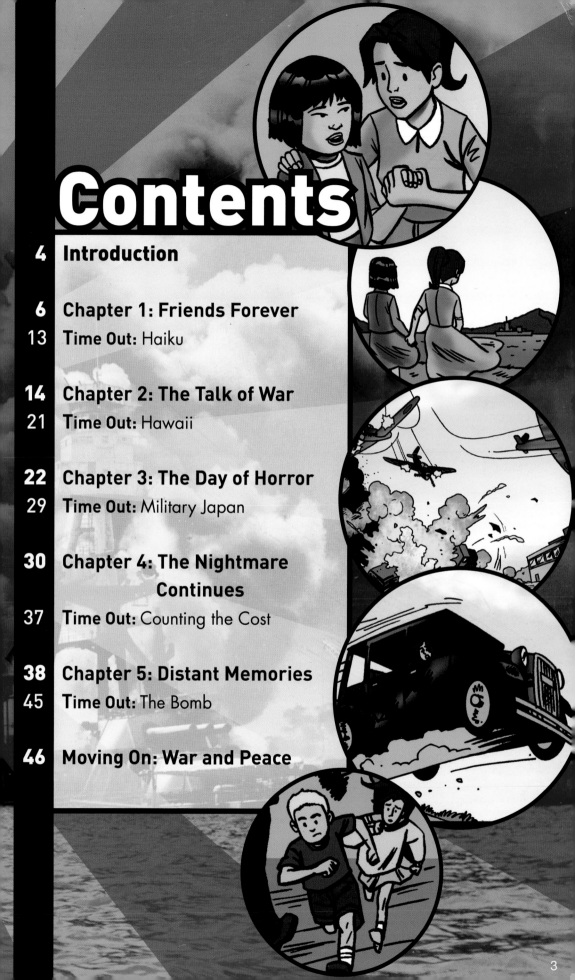

In the 1930s, Japan became a powerful military force. By 1940, Japan was on the march. It expanded its empire to China and was preparing for war in Eastern Asia and the Pacific region.

Japanese invasion of China

The United States stopped its sale of oil to Japan in 1940, hoping to halt Japan's advance. In late 1941, a big fleet of U.S. warships anchored at Pearl Harbor. Pearl Harbor was a naval base on Oahu, one of the main islands of Hawaii.

Attack on Pearl Harbor

TIMELINE

1937 »	Dec. 7, 1941 »	Dec. 8, 1941 »	Feb. 1942 »	June 1942 »
Japan invades China.	Japan attacks Pearl Harbor. War in the Pacific begins.	Japan attacks Malaya and the Philippines. The United States and Britain declare war on Japan.	The British troops in Singapore surrender to the Japanese army.	The United States defeats Japan in the Battle of Midway.

4

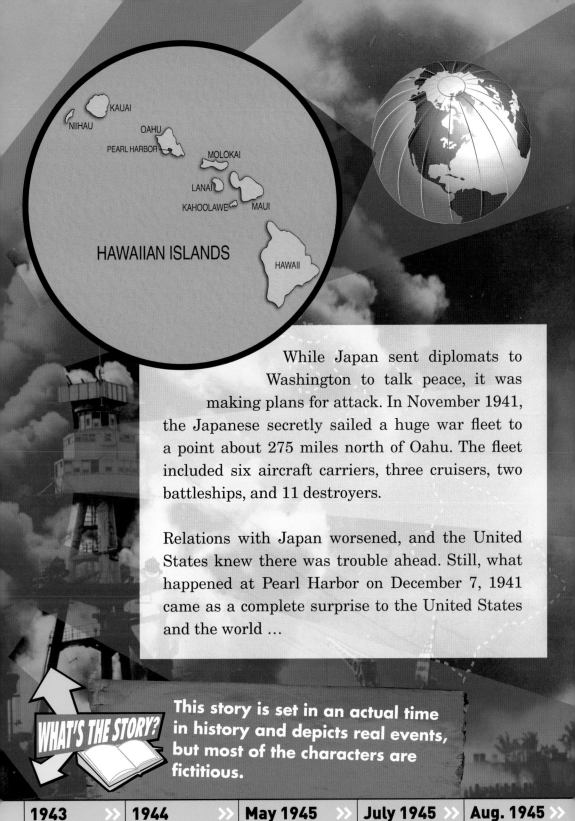

KAUAI

NIIHAU

OAHU

PEARL HARBOR

MOLOKAI

LANAI

KAHOOLAWE   MAUI

HAWAIIAN ISLANDS

HAWAII

While Japan sent diplomats to Washington to talk peace, it was making plans for attack. In November 1941, the Japanese secretly sailed a huge war fleet to a point about 275 miles north of Oahu. The fleet included six aircraft carriers, three cruisers, two battleships, and 11 destroyers.

Relations with Japan worsened, and the United States knew there was trouble ahead. Still, what happened at Pearl Harbor on December 7, 1941 came as a complete surprise to the United States and the world …

WHAT'S THE STORY?

This story is set in an actual time in history and depicts real events, but most of the characters are fictitious.

1943	1944	May 1945	July 1945	Aug. 1945
The United States begins to win the war in the Pacific region.	The Japanese air force uses kamikaze (suicide) attacks.	The Allies win victory in Europe.	The first atomic bomb is tested in the United States.	The United States drops atomic bombs on Hiroshima and Nagasaki. Japan surrenders.

BACK AT HOME ...

ALISON! COME AND MEET DR. FUJIRO OBASAN, YOUR GODFATHER.

I HAVE A GODFATHER?

DR. OBASAN? CAN HE BE THE FAMOUS WRITER WHO'S COMING TO MY SCHOOL?

HELLO, ALISON. YOUR MOTHER WROTE TO ME WHEN YOU WERE BORN, ASKING ME TO BE YOUR GODFATHER. I NEVER HAD A CHANCE TO VISIT UNTIL NOW.

FUJIRO LIVED FAR AWAY AND HE TRAVELED A LOT. AFTER YOUR MOTHER STOPPED WRITING TO HIM, WE DIDN'T THINK IT WAS IMPORTANT TO TELL YOU ABOUT YOUR JAPANESE GODFATHER!

ALISON, THIS IS MY DAUGHTER JASMINE. SHE IS 12, LIKE YOU.

KONNICHIWA! HELLO, ALISON.

HI, JASMINE. YOU SPEAK ENGLISH!

10

HAIKU

Haiku is a form of Japanese poem that is extremely brief but very powerful. Haiku are only three lines long, but they create a sense of wonder about everyday things. Haiku are very popular in the West and are often written in English.

Old pond
Frog jumps in
Splash!

This autumn
Why am I aging so?
Flying towards the clouds, a bird.

Will you start a fire?
I'll show you something nice —
A huge snowball.

Haiku by Basho,
translated into English

The most famous haiku poet was Matsuo Basho (1644–1694). He wrote beautiful haiku about nature and the passing of time.

HAWAII

Hawaii is made up of many islands. The main islands are Hawaii, Oahu, Kauai, and Maui. These islands are actually the tops of undersea volcanoes! The capital of Hawaii is Honolulu, on the island of Oahu. Pearl Harbor is 4 miles west of Honolulu.

The first people to live in Hawaii were the Polynesians. Later, many other groups arrived from Japan, China, the Philippines, Europe, and the United States. Hawaii became a territory of the United States in 1900. The naval base at Pearl Harbor was built in 1908.

Hawaii became the 50th U.S. state in 1959. It is a popular vacation spot, as well as a leading producer of sugar cane and pineapples.

The islands of Hawaii are the most isolated in the world. It is a very long plane ride from anywhere to Hawaii. There is plenty of time to memorize the spelling of the Hawaiian state fish called the *humuhumunukunukuapua'a!*

Kilauea Volcano in Hawaii

TIME OUT!

The Japanese attack on Pearl Harbor was part of a larger plan. The Japanese had invaded China in 1937. They wished to build an empire in Asia.

At almost the same time as the Japanese Air Force bombed Pearl Harbor, Japanese troops landed on the beaches of Malaya in Southeast Asia. Japan continued to invade and occupy many countries in Southeast Asia, including Thailand, Malaysia, Singapore, the Philippines, and Indonesia.

After Pearl Harbor, Admiral Yamamoto, who planned the attack, was said to have warned his emperor that "we have awakened a sleeping giant."

Japanese war poster

The attack on Pearl Harbor became a big problem for Japanese-Americans. The U.S. government placed more than 120,000 Japanese-Americans in camps in lonely locations throughout the country during the war.

THE USS *WEST VIRGINIA* AND *TENNESSEE* ARE DANGEROUSLY CLOSE TO THE *ARIZONA*. THE *TENNESSEE* TAKES TWO DIRECT HITS, BUT IT DOES NOT SINK.

THE CREW OF THE *WEST VIRGINIA* IS ORDERED TO ABANDON SHIP.

THAT'S MY DAD'S SHIP! DADDY ...

8:15 A.M. FLEET SHIPS OPEN FIRE ON ENEMY AIRCRAFT. THE SKIES FILL WITH DENSE BLACK SMOKE!

BY THIS TIME, THE SHOCK GIVES WAY TO ANGER AND DETERMINATION.

8:30 A.M. THE SECOND WAVE OF THE ATTACK BEGINS.

QUICK, ALISON! THE ATTACK IS STARTING AGAIN. WE'VE GOT TO GET TO THE FERRY.

FERRY OFFICE

OH NO! THE FERRY IS DAMAGED! WE CAN'T GET TO FORD ISLAND.

COUNTING THE COST

TIME OUT!

The USS Arizona Memorial in Pearl Harbor

At the time of the attack, the United States had more than half of its Pacific fleet in Pearl Harbor. On hearing of the attack, President Roosevelt ordered the Army and Navy to "FIGHT BACK!" Here are some of the losses suffered that day:

PERSONNEL
- The U.S. lost 2,341 servicemen and 49 civilians.
- Japan lost 64 servicemen.

SHIPS
- Twelve U.S. ships were sunk and nine damaged.
- The USS *Arizona* was hit by a 1,760-lb. bomb. It sank in less than nine minutes, killing 1,177 crewmen.
- There were 334 survivors from the USS *Arizona*. As these men die, their ashes are placed in the USS Arizona Memorial.
- Japan lost five ships.

AIRCRAFT
- U.S. Air Force: 164 planes destroyed, 159 damaged.
- Japanese Air Force: 29 planes destroyed, 74 damaged.

9:00 A.M. THE SECOND WAVE OF THE ATTACK CONTINUES. THE *HONOLULU* IS BADLY DAMAGED, AND THE *PENNSYLVANIA* CATCHES FIRE.

THIS IS THE BERTH OF DADDY'S SHIP. BUT ... WH–WHERE'S THE SHIP?

OH NO, BUDDY! IT HAS SUNK!

THE MEN OF THE *ARIZONA* WOULD NEVER SEE THEIR FAMILIES AGAIN.

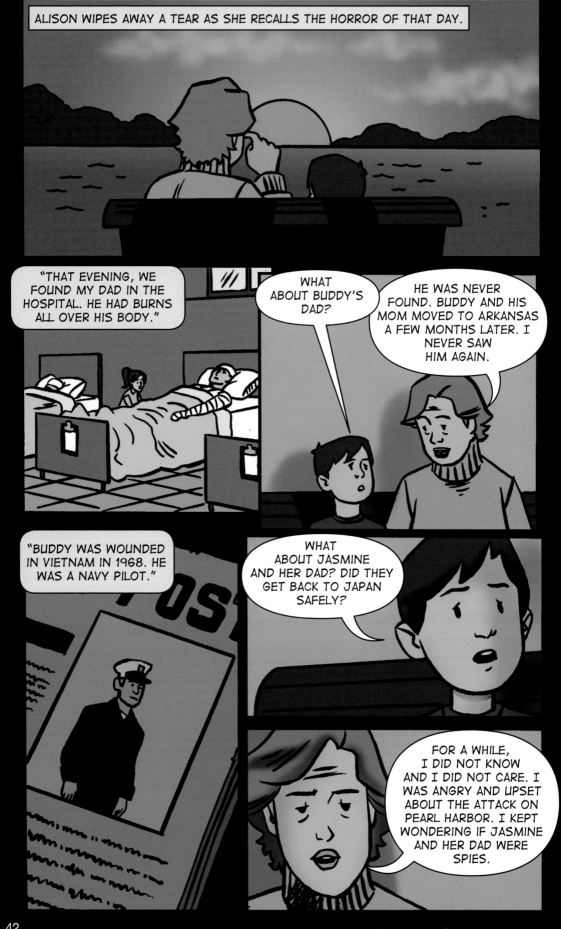

ALISON WIPES AWAY A TEAR AS SHE RECALLS THE HORROR OF THAT DAY.

"THAT EVENING, WE FOUND MY DAD IN THE HOSPITAL. HE HAD BURNS ALL OVER HIS BODY."

WHAT ABOUT BUDDY'S DAD?

HE WAS NEVER FOUND. BUDDY AND HIS MOM MOVED TO ARKANSAS A FEW MONTHS LATER. I NEVER SAW HIM AGAIN.

"BUDDY WAS WOUNDED IN VIETNAM IN 1968. HE WAS A NAVY PILOT."

WHAT ABOUT JASMINE AND HER DAD? DID THEY GET BACK TO JAPAN SAFELY?

FOR A WHILE, I DID NOT KNOW AND I DID NOT CARE. I WAS ANGRY AND UPSET ABOUT THE ATTACK ON PEARL HARBOR. I KEPT WONDERING IF JASMINE AND HER DAD WERE SPIES.

THE BOMB

After Pearl Harbor, the United States declared war against Japan and Germany. On the morning of August 6, 1945, an atom bomb nicknamed "Little Boy" was dropped on the Japanese city of Hiroshima. The bomb exploded 1,900 feet above ground. The shock wave destroyed everything within a 1.5 mile radius. A terrible firestorm burned an area of 5 square miles. Up to 180,000 people died, out of a population of 350,000.

On August 8, the United States dropped another atom bomb, nicknamed "Fat Man," on the city of Nagasaki. Six days later, Japan accepted unconditional surrender.

People still disagree about whether it was necessary to kill so many innocent Japanese people in these two cities. Some argue that it should never have been done. Others say that it was the only way to make Japan surrender and to prevent more deaths.

WAR AND

A group of children, including those of Japanese descent, say the Pledge of Allegiance.

PEACE

Pearl Harbor is a significant event in the history of the United States of America. It brought the country into the war against both Germany and Japan.

In the four years of war against the United States, the Japanese people lost nearly everything. More than 2.6 million Japanese people died in World War II. Almost 100,000 U.S. troops were killed.

The Allies occupied Japan from 1945 to 1952. They brought democracy and stripped the Emperor of his powers.

After the war, Commander Mitsuo Fuchida said he was sorry for what the Japanese had done at Pearl Harbor. For the rest of his life, he preached a message of peace.

The U.S. and Japan have been strong allies since the end of World War II. Today, young people in Japan like to watch American movies and listen to American pop music. Young people in the U.S. are interested in Japanese animé, martial arts, and food.

INDEX